What It Takes...
To Earn $1,000,000 in
Direct Sales

Million Dollar Achievers Reveal The Secrets To Becoming
Wildly Successful.

by Kirsten McCay-Smith

50 Interviews: Women Millionaires
What It Takes...To Earn $1,000,000 in Direct Sales
Copyright © 2009 by Kirsten McCay-Smith
millionaires.50interviews.com

ISBN 978-0-9822907-4-3

Published by
Wise Media Group
444 17th Street, Suite 507
Denver, CO 80202

First edition.
Printed in the United States of America.

Wise Media Group
Denver, CO

This book is dedicated to all the women in direct sales who won't give up...no matter what!!

I want to thank all my friends on Facebook who gave me the ideas and connections to make these interviews possible. A special thanks to Cheryl Anderson for all her time and commitment to MY project.

"Opportunities are usually disguised as hard work, so most people don't recognize them."
- Ann Landers

FOREWORD

Chances are, if you are hiking up a mountain trail, you'll exchange information with others on their way down. They may offer you helpful suggestions about upcoming obstacles, or point out sights to enjoy which you may have missed on your own. Maybe you'll stop them to ask for more detailed information. In these exchanges, you've enriched your own journey while offering others a chance to make a positive difference.

Sharing the collective wisdom of individuals who are successful in their endeavors is the greater purpose of 50 Interviews.

Kirsten McCay-Smith is driven to uncover the secrets to making it big in direct selling and network marketing. By reading her book, you will get a glimpse of what she discovered.

In this first volume of *What it Takes To Earn $1,000,000 in Direct Sales*, Kirsten offers exclusive interviews with women who have already achieved unusual levels of success. In doing so, she shares the unwritten rules, exposes the myths, and reveals new truths about what it takes for you to become wildly successful yourself!

The interviews expose the simple fact that those who are most successful, must first and foremost – love what they do.

The magic of these structured interviews is that they lead us to discover our own answers from within. These conversations between the interviewer and the interviewee result in truths for each of those women. As the reader, you bring yet another perspective, and reveal new truths. I encourage you to share these interviews with others. Each time you do, you will develop a new level of understanding and appreciation for the treasure and tool in your hands. I also encourage you to re-read these interviews periodically. The personal experiences you have between readings may result in you finding new relevance each time you review them, and the value of your investment will increase each time you do so.

On a final note, the changes I have seen in Kirsten through her process of conducting these interviews are nothing short of dramatic. I want to express my sincere gratitude to all those participants who were gracious enough to share an hour of their time with her. In turn, she and the other authors of the *50 Interviews* series of books, are doing a great service to the world by sharing their interviews with you.

All my best to your continued success,
Brian Schwartz
Catalyst
50 Interviews Inc.

TABLE OF CONTENTS

INTRODUCTION

Before starting my direct sales business with a fabulous romance party plan, I spent fifteen years in the fitness industry as a successful fitness instructor and personal trainer. I wasn't a morning person and had to work every morning at 5am to accommodate people's work schedules. I began to get frustrated because I wanted my clients to be healthier than they wanted to be. It was even more frustrating to realize that no matter how hard I worked, my income always remained the same. I was working 60 hours a week and at the top of the pay scale in the fitness world. I was worn out and there was no room for growth. I felt stuck!

Once I transitioned to direct sales, I realized that I was finally in the driver seat of my own professional and financial success. I could choose when to work – no more trudging to the gym in the wee hours of the morning – and I could choose how many hours to put in each week. I worked really hard and I was finally able to see a direct correlation between my efforts and my earning potential. Four years later, I still jump out of bed later in the day, eager to develop myself, serve my customers, and provide support to my large team of consultants.

So, why bother to do 50 interviews?

There is an adage that says, "If you want to get somewhere in life, find someone who has already paved the way and follow in their footsteps." In this case, I set out to talk to 50 women who have earned a million dollars or more through direct sales. I wanted to learn from their experiences and dispel some of the myths about multi-level marketing. I was looking for confirmation that I was on the right career path and I hoped to gain new insights to inspire my down line.

The interview process confirmed one thing that I knew all along.

Nothing worth achieving in this life comes easily. Every one of these wildly successful women were quick to point out that it took hard work to achieve financial success. Direct sales is not about earning easy money and success doesn't happen overnight. But, if you are willing to work hard, there is virtually no limit to the financial and personal rewards you can obtain.

I truly believe that this is the BEST industry in the world! Think about it. I never have to worry about being laid off. Studies show that sales in this industry remain steady in good and bad economic times. Direct sales can help you achieve your financial goals whether you are looking to earn discretionary cash or to drastically increase your net worth.

I set my schedule. I decide when I want to be promoted and take on more responsibility. I can choose to close up shop and take an extended vacation. Or, I can throw my heart and soul into my business, and do what it takes to earn a million dollars. The best part is that I am empowering other women every step of the way. I have found my passion! I invite you to read on to learn if direct selling is the right path for you. If it is, dig deeper into these interviews to find what it takes to make a million and how you can use their experience and wisdom to guide your path!

"You need to go fishing everyday because you never know when you're going to catch a big one."

Ellen Annis, Tupperware

◆

BACKGROUND

After a car accident ended her 16 year career as a Colorado licensed electrician, Ellen Annis started selling Tupperware. At first, she joined just so her friend would get a gift from the company, but after seeing some immediate success, she was hooked. She called in sick to her job so she could go to her first convention. After that, there was no stopping her. She returned to her job and started making phone calls on breaks and the rest is history! Ellen has been with Tupperware for 15 years and has enjoyed 17 paid vacations and 11 different company vehicles. Ellen is 49 years old, and lives in Englewood, CO.

INTERVIEW

Q: What year was the company founded?
A: 1946.

Q: What year did you start with the company?
A: 1994.

Q: Why did you choose this company in particular?
A: I loved the product and signed up for the discount and to help a friend win a prize. My friend helped me pay for my kit and I used the profit from my first catalog sales to pay her back. I hid it from my husband in the beginning. He really wasn't supportive until the new TV arrived.

Q: Did you have previous experience in direct sales?

ELLEN ANNIS

A: No.

Q: What were you doing before this?
A: I was an electrician for over 16 years, owning my own business for the last five. I was in a disabling car accident and had to give it up.

Q: Did you choose the direct sales model on purpose?
A: No, I only wanted a discount on the product.

Q: How many hours a week do you work now?
A: 25, but it never feels like work. I always say, "When I go to work I end up at a party."

Q: How about when you first got started?
A: I did a lot more at first. I worked 50-60 hours a week to build the business and get it to where it is today.

Q: Do you set goals? Do you write them down?
A: Yes. You have to write them down...they are the road map to your success.

Q: How long did it take you to make $1,000,000?
A: 10 years.

Q: What did that look like?
A: I made $50,000 in my second year and it has gone up every year since.

Q: Was it your intention to make $1,000,000?
A: No, not even to make it into a career. My intention was to get a discount on the product I love.

Q: When you first started, did you think you would be this successful?
A: Not at first, but when I started seeing success right away, I knew I was hooked. I was drawn to the recognition I would

TUPPERWARE

2

get from the company for my accomplishments, as well as the ease of my success.

Q: What do you attribute your success to?

A: I listened to my upline and did what they told me to do. I followed a system, set goals, and did the work. I look for new people all the time to join me in my business. I don't dwell on people who don't want to have a party or join the business, I just move on, there are so many people out there!

> *"I don't dwell on people who don't want to have a party or join the business, I just move on, there are so many people out there!"*

Q: What techniques have you found to be successful in recruiting others?

A: I love personal contact and building a relationship with potential consultants. Finding out what they really want out of the business and out of life, helps me know if I can help give them what they want.

Q: How do you keep your team motivated?

A: Constant communication in all forms such as mail, email, phone, and meetings. I always match their energy, commitment, and actions.

Q: What have been your greatest challenges and how have you overcome them?

A: My greatest challenge definitely would be time management and how to get my business to work around my family life. I overcame this by sitting down with my family and sharing my goals and my vision, which included a better life for all of us. Now I work with the family, we set schedules together. My family is my first priority. Always make a plan and a schedule and work it.

ELLEN ANNIS

Q: How has your success changed your life?

A: I lost 100 pounds. I learned how to cook and learned proper nutrition. I now have the time and resources to cook healthy meals. I also have time to get my exercise and relaxation in.

Q: Is there anything else you want to share?

A: Don't be afraid and be patient. Take little bits and pieces at a time. Be consistent. Be passionate about your product, use your product, and share your business with everyone. Your business is built one grain of sand at a time. This foundation of great customers, hosts, and team members, will make your business a solid and successful one, just like cement!

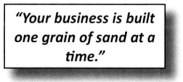

"Your business is built one grain of sand at a time."

TUPPERWARE

"If you love what you do and do what you love, you will never work a day in your life."
Christa Aufdemberg, Pre-Paid Legal

◆

BACKGROUND

Christa always knew she wanted to be her own boss and make her own hours with an unlimited income potential. Thanks to her great team and working with her two best friends in the business, she has accomplished that. In 1998 Christa received the *Emerging Entrepreneur of the Year* award from the National Association of Women Business Owners (NAWBO). She was featured in the March 2000 issue of *Orange Coast* magazine and in 2001 she was inducted into the NAWBO's Hall of Fame for Remarkable Women. She is the Senior Vice President of Group Marketing for California and was the 6th top producer in the company in 2005. She is also the first single woman and single mother to be a 250K Ring Earner. Christa has personally sold over 7,000 memberships, is currently the 16th top producer in the entire company for 2008, and is a Millionaire Club Member. Christa continues to enjoy a lifestyle that most people only dream of – working for herself but not by herself. "I have no hidden talents. I want to inspire, motivate, and continue to educate women across this nation that if I can do it with no business or networking background as a single mother, you can too." She tells all new associates this is a relationship business. "Duplication is the key. Do what successful people do. Kathryn Walden, a pioneer in group marketing said it the best with a K.I.S.S. – KEEP IT SIMPLE, SILLY!" Christa is 40 years old, and lives in Tustin, CA.

INTERVIEW

Q: What year was the company founded?
A: 1972.

Q: What year did you start with the company?
A: 1996.

Q: Why did you choose this company in particular?
A: I had a strong belief in the product. It was something everyone needed and could afford.

Q: Did you have previous experience in direct sales?
A: No.

Q: What were you doing before this?
A: I was an office manager at a doctor's office, before that I was a college student.

Q: Did you choose the direct sales model on purpose?
A: No, I just liked the product, the flexibility, and the income potential.

Q: How many hours per week do you work now?
A: Approximately 25 hours.

Q: How about when you first got started?
A: Approximately 10. I had two kids that kept me busy.

Q: Do you set goals? Do you write them down?
A: Yes, I keep a daily "to do" list. I write down daily actions and I have a dream board.

Q: How long did it take you to make $1,000,000?
A: 10 years.

Q: What did that look like?
A: The first year I made $19,000, and it doubled over the next

four years. By my sixth year I was making over $100,000 and by my eighth year $250,000.

Q: Was it your intention to make $1,000,000?

A: I initially wanted to make $500-$1,000 each month to stay home with my kids. After the third month of working with Pre-Paid Legal, I quit my full time job.

> *"My driving force was people saying I couldn't do it and I wanted to prove them wrong."*

Q: When you first started, did you think you would be this successful?

A: No, I thought it would be a part time supplement to my household income. I didn't believe in myself and didn't believe I was capable of this kind of success. Direct sales is about personal development, and I had to have someone else believe in me until I could believe in myself. I finally started to believe in myself in my third year and wanted to mentor and help others do the same.

Q: What do you attribute your success to?

A: Initially, I was driven by proving to the skeptics that I could do it. My driving force was people saying I couldn't do it and I wanted to prove them wrong. I kept with it. After making enough money, it became more about helping women and single parents. To motivate, inspire, and educate them; to teach something that is simple and can be duplicated.

Q: What techniques have you found to be successful in recruiting others?

A: I find out how I can help them achieve their dreams.

Q: How do you keep your team motivated?

A: Plugging them into the system and teaching them to be dependent on the system. I treat them like family and work more with people who feel the same way as I do. I always match their effort.

CHRISTA AUFDEMBERG

Q: What have been your greatest challenges and how did you overcome them?

A: I thought I was entitled to a successful business instead of knowing I had to help others to be successful. I overcame this through personal development and getting to know myself. I learned that the more people I help, the more abundant I will be. Everything changed when I started helping others.

Q: How has making $1,000,000 changed your life?

A: How hasn't it? I get a lot of recognition from the company, which I love. It gives me the credibility to inspire others. I have also remodeled my house, I drive a Mercedes, I send my kids to private school. I have time, freedom, and unlimited choices.

> *"Find something you're passionate about."*

Q: Is there anything else you want to share?

A: I am thankful I am making the same amount of money I have been for the past few years and I can't be laid off. As the economy is changing, this is the perfect time to look into direct sales. Find something you're passionate about. If there's a market for it, the price is right, the company has credibility, you don't quit, and you have fun, you will be successful! At the end of every meeting I say, "If you love what you do and do what you love, you will never work a day in your life."

PRE-PAID LEGAL

3

"If people like you and trust you they will be customers for life."

Risa Barash, Fairy Tales Hair Care

◆

BACKGROUND

Risa Barash was a successful stand-up comedian in her native Manhattan area before entering the world of direct sales. She married in 2000 and soon thereafter, took her husband's idea of creating hair care products for children that prevent head lice. She created Fairy Tales Hair Care, infused with organic herbs of rosemary, citronella, tea tree and lavender. She began selling to small beauty supply stores, salons and pharmacies. A year later she launched her website. Risa is now proud to be known as "the lice lady". Fairy Tales has grown into a multimillion dollar business and the line has expanded to include lice removal products and bed bug sprays. As an expert on all things lice, Risa is proud to be an educator on lice and lice prevention, as well as a spokesperson for Fairy Tales. She has helped tens of thousands of parents see the lighter side of head lice, and claims all it takes is a good metal nit removal comb and a great bottle of wine. Risa is 43 years old, and lives in Wayne, NJ.

INTERVIEW

Q: What year was the company founded?
A: 1999.

Q: What year did you start with the company?
A: 1999.

Q: Why did you choose this company in particular?
A: I started the company. A family member owned a children's

hair care salon and there were lots of kids coming in with lice and no good products to cure it.

Q: Did you have previous experience in direct sales?
A: No.

Q: What were you doing before this?
A: I started out in public relations. I worked for a big New York City PR firm. I quit to chase my dream of becoming a stand-up comic, which I did for six years.

> *"I was raising two kids so I could only work the business part time."*

Q: Did you choose the direct sales model on purpose?
A: Yes, I started by selling direct to salons, then to moms on the internet, and now I use distributors to sell the products.

Q: How many hours a week do you work now?
A: A minimum of 50.

Q: How about when you first got started?
A: Less when I started, I started slow. I was raising two kids so I could only work the business part time.

Q: Do you set goals? Do you write them down?
A: Absolutely. I find it fun to make a checklist every day and cross them off the checklist.

Q: How long did it take you to make $1,000,000?
A: Four years.

Q: What did that look like?
A: In the first year, I made $200,000 direct selling to salons. Then after two years, I added distributors and it took off from there. Profits doubled almost every year.

Q: Was it your intention to make $1,000,000?

FAIRY TALES HAIR CARE

A: Yes, absolutely!

Q: When you first started, did you think you would be this successful?
A: Yes, I knew I was on to something really good. I filled a niche, a void in the market. I made a point to build brand identity and brand loyalty.

Q: What do you attribute your success to?
A: I have a great product, amazing customer service, and will do what it takes to be successful. I train everyone else to do the same exact thing. I am also able to attribute my success to word of mouth. When people like you they tell their friends, personality is huge.

> *"It has given me the freedom to take care of my kids and make sure they have everything they need."*

Q: What techniques have you found to be successful in recruiting others?
A: I educate all our distributors and only work with people who are established, motivated and have sales experience.

Q: How do you keep your team motivated?
A: I am always coming up with great new products. I am also there for them for anything they need.

Q: What have been your greatest challenges and how did you overcome them?
A: Staying focused. It is easy to expand into other markets or products to sell more stuff, but I just tell myself, "Stick with the plan." I stick with the products that build my brand and stay with my mission.

Q: How has making $1,000,000 changed your life?
A: It has given me the freedom to take care of my kids and make

RISA BARASH

sure they have everything they need. And…I'm a shoe person…enough said!

Q: Is there anything else you want to share?

A: <u>Just stick with it and stay focused.</u> I pride myself on my customer service. "It's so odd that you and I have become friends through lice," is something that I hear often. I have given away a lot of free stuff. I am constantly sending out free products and giving away samples at the hair shows. If people like you and trust you, they will be customers for life.

FAIRY TALES HAIR CARE

4

"I love that I can help people who are struggling, because I used to be one of those who needed the help. This industry is the best way to make a difference in this world."

Cindy Heugly, Isagenix

◆

BACKGROUND

Cindy Hueghly is the newest millionaire in Isagenix and was featured on the cover of the company's *New Wealth* brochure. Her success story has been featured in *Success from Home* magazine and *Utah Valley Magazine*. She received the prestigious award of "Outstanding Women of Isagenix" in 2006 when she was also recognized for being one of the top 25 income earners that year. Cindy is a stay-at-home mom with six kids. She was able to retire her husband three years ago at age 36. Cindy is currently a trainer for Isagenix. She is 37 years old, and lives in American Fork, UT.

INTERVIEW

Q: What year was the company founded?
A: 2002.

Q: What year did you start with the company?
A: 2002.

Q: Why did you choose this company in particular?
A: My husband had just been laid off and we moved in with my parents, whose home was in foreclosure. A distributor called my dad, who was already in network marketing, and told him about the business opportunity with Isagenix. He

was more interested in the products so we both started with the products. I lost a lot of weight and saw an increase in my health. The products changed my life, so I just started sharing them with everyone. After I had been using products for a while, I thought I may be able to earn some extra income for my family.

> *"I liked the idea of having no boss, no commutes, setting my own hours..."*

Q: Did you have previous experience in direct sales?
A: No, none at all.

Q: What were you doing before this?
A: I was a stay at home mom with six kids.

Q: Did you choose the direct sales model on purpose?
A: Not really, but my dad had been in multi-level marketing for over 27 years so I believed in the concept. I liked the idea of having no boss, no commutes, setting my own hours, no education barriers, and I love the fact that it is people helping people. If you help enough people reach their goals, you will automatically reach your own goals.

Q: How many hours per week do you work now?
A: 20.

Q: How about when you first got started?
A: About 30 hours a week plus some weekends. My role has changed from recruiting to working with my team.

Q: Do you set goals? Do you write them down?
A: I do now. When I started seeing money come in, my belief level increased and I started setting small goals. I wanted to pay cash for a piano, and did. I then started making bigger and bigger goals. I wanted to retire my husband, and I did. I write everything down. I write exactly how much I want to make in a year and then I break it down into weekly goals

ISAGENIIX

and actions. What am I going to do every single day to move my business forward?

Q: How long did it take you to make $1,000,000?
A: Six years.

Q: What did that look like?
A: The first year I made $45,000. In my third year I was still under $100,000, and then my fourth year I jumped to over $200,000. I was motivated to make more money to prove to everyone that I could.

Q: Was it your intention to make $1,000,000?
A: I don't think it was. That never really crossed my mind. Not until I was about to make a million dollars. I actually surprised myself!

Q: When you first started, did you think you would be this successful?
A: I hoped I would be. I remember talking to someone who was a millionaire in Isagenix and my belief level wasn't quite there yet. I had to change some of my thoughts and words I used with myself. One of the greatest things I have achieved is self growth and personal development. The question is, "Who do you need to become to make a million dollars?" My dad always said, "Work harder on yourself than you do on your business."

> *"Work harder on yourself than you do on your business."*

Q: What do you attribute your success to?
A: I would say being coachable and willing to follow a system that is already put in place. People go out and try to reinvent the wheel instead of watching and doing what the successful people are already doing. I was like a sponge, I was teachable. You have to be willing to do what it takes.

Q: What techniques have you found to be successful in recruiting others?

A: I use in home presentations working with other people's warm markets. I always book at least one more home presentation from each one. I find this easy to duplicate. You have to be able to duplicate yourself to grow your business.

Q: How do you keep your team motivated?

A: I run contests for my team. I have taken them on cruises, dinner in a limo, etc.

Q: What have been your greatest challenges and how have you overcome them?

A: In the beginning when my kids were little (my kids were 1 ½-7 years old), getting them to see the bigger picture and have them see my vision so they would support all the hours I was putting in to my business was a challenge. So I sat down with my kids and told them what I wanted, for their father to retire and be at home with them all day. I had them visualize what they wanted to do and to have, and what it would be like to have their dad at home. Once they saw why I was doing this, they were all on board and we all worked together. It was also a challenge getting my husband to believe that I could be successful in network marketing. When he started seeing the money come in, his belief started to increase. Sometimes he still can't believe that I make this much.

> *"I run contests for my team. I have taken them on cruises, dinner in a limo, etc."*

Q: How has making $1,000,000 changed your life?

A: All my kids are in lots of extracurricular activities, my husband gets to do what he loves, and most importantly we have so much freedom with our time. I bought my husband his dream car for Father's Day last year, it was fun.

Q: Is there anything else you want to share?

ISAGENIX

A: This is the best industry in the world. It gives people the freedom to live their lives and not have to worry about money, it is residual income. Get involved in network marketing because of how many lives you can change. I never apologize for the money I earn in the company. I know every dollar I have made has been from helping someone's health or someone's financial situation. If you act as if you are successful, you will see success faster. Most people don't believe in themselves enough in the beginning.

> *"Failing is not in falling down, it is in staying down."*

You can't feed the poor if you are one. I wanted to give but I didn't even have enough for my own family. Now I am in the position where I can give. I love that I can help people who are struggling because I used to be one of those who needed the help. This industry is the best way to make a difference in this world.

Never give up. Failing is not in falling down, it is in staying down.

CINDY HEUGLY

"One of the many benefits of leadership is that while the team grows, the leader must also grow."

Jan Moestue, Passion Parties

◆

BACKGROUND

Jan Moestue was formerly the controller at the Passion Parties corporate office. She saw the checks that were going out to the leaders of the company and realized the awesome potential of being a consultant and owning her own Passion Parties business. She left the corporate world of Passion Parties to join as a consultant. During the next twelve years, she built an organization of thousands of business women who sell several million dollars in product every year. Jan has earned top leadership awards including the Home Award and the Car Award, and has been number one in organizational sales and organizational sponsoring in the company. Jan is 53 years old, and lives in Oakland, CA.

INTERVIEW

Q: What year was the company founded?
A: 1994.

Q: What year did you start with the company?
A: 1996.

Q: Why did you choose this company in particular?
A: I actually started as a contract bookkeeper with the mail order company that turned into Passion Parties. When it turned into Passion Parties in 1994, I became an employee. I wanted to be a stay-at-home mom and saw some of the checks that were going out to the consultants and thought I

would give it a try...mostly out of curiosity.

Q: Did you have previous experience in direct sales?
A: When I was 18 I did a very short time with Avon, almost nothing.

Q: Did you choose the direct sales model on purpose?
A: No, I was from the mail order world and didn't understand

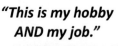

"This is my hobby AND my job."

the sales model. I couldn't figure out why the consultants who all owned their own businesses needed so much encouragement, support, and recognition. I didn't buy into the down line concept. I chose it as, "I'll give this a try to give myself a break from accounting for a year."

Q: How many hours per week do you work now?
A: I am a workaholic so I work as much as I can, definitely more than 40, but not because I have to, because I want to. This is my hobby AND my job.

Q: How about when you first got started?
A: The first year I stayed on as a consulting controller so I was only building my business part time. The second year I started picking it up and working about the same number of hours as now, just working it very differently.

Q: Do you set goals? Do you write them down?
A: Yes.

Q: How long did it take you to make $1,000,000?
A: Nine and a half years.

Q: What did that look like?
A: The first year I made $800, then it tripled each year for about six years, and then it "slowed" to doubling in the last four years.

PASSION PARTIES

Q: Was it your intention to make $1,000,000?

A: No, I actually didn't have a belief in the direct sales model. I didn't believe that it was possible.

Q: When you first started, did you think you would be this successful?

A: No, not at first. I didn't think that direct selling was the right model for wealth like that. I had a belief in myself, not just the compensation plan.

Q: What do you attribute your success to?

A: The party plan business is clearly a relationship and numbers business. I am lucky because I can understand both of those. I come from a numbers background and I have a lot of patience and tenacity, two very important personality traits for success in this business.

Q: What techniques have you found to be successful in recruiting others?

A: Recruiting a new consultant is a very short term relationship while leading is a very long term relationship, so I focus more on leading than recruiting. I am genuine and I believe I am helping every single person I sponsor in the business. I believe they are going to get something good out of it.

Q: How do you keep your team motivated?

A: I speak to my team as a unit so they have a sense of unity and belonging. I deal with my first level as a separate team, in their own entity, and run monthly contests for both my first level and my entire team. I am easy to approach and I am fair.

> " ...I focus more on leading than recruiting."

Q: What have been your greatest challenges and how have you overcome them?

A: I learn more and more every single year and the challenge is

JAN MOESTUE

to keep it simple for my team and my new consultants. It has to be able to be duplicated. This year I have concentrated more on simplifying the party process and I constantly talk with the other top leaders to discuss ways to make the business simpler and easier for others. It's too easy to get creative and complicated, so just keep it simple and systemize everything!

Q: How has making $1,000,000 changed your life?
A: I believe whatever drove you to make your money will be what you use your money on. My kids are my focus. I started to be a stay-at-home mom with my kids and now I do whatever I want with and for my kids. Money solves many parenting problems. My kids went to private school and now I have a rental house that they can live in when they're ready. It's almost all for my kids.

Q: Is there anything else you want to share?
A: Party plan is the way to go. The thought of selling one-on-one seems painfully challenging. With party plan, you have an audience of 8-15 people at a time and you have a built in referral system. You're booking parties from parties, and sponsoring new consultants from your parties. I can't understand why anyone would go to a one-on-one sale with no referral system.

You have to have an incredible amount of patience. This is not a get rich quick scheme. It does have the potential to make a huge amount of money by doing exactly what you're doing now with no further formal education, just practice and patience. On a numbers and dollars level, this just makes sense!

"I can have fun now and make contributions to others."

Bonnie Perkins, Isagenix

◆

BACKGROUND

Bonnie Perkins is a retired hair dresser of 34 years. She also re-tired her husband, Paul, through her business and loves spending time with her family, including two children, and four grandchildren. Bonnie is grateful for her health. Her hobbies include gardening, exercising, and running half marathons. She loves the sun and the outdoors, but most of all loves what she does regularly – meeting people and building relationships. Bonnie loves seeing her team grow and achieve greatness. Even more so, she loves seeing them achieve their dreams and goals. Bonnie was nominated for an Outstanding Woman of 2005 award with Isagenix. She is also featured in a book with four of her business partners, *Say Be Go Do* by Tiffany Rhoades. Bonnie is 61 years old, and lives in Layton, UT.

INTERVIEW

Q: What year was the company founded?
A: 2002.

Q: What year did you start with the company?
A: 2002.

Q: Why did you choose this company in particular?
A: I had someone call me from a previous company I was with about the product. I was looking for a product that would make me feel better because I had a lot of health challenges. I had great results so of course I told everyone. About six

months into it, I realized it was a business.

Q: Did you have previous experience in direct sales?
A: Yes, I was with a company in 1989, just for the product. I told everyone I was always looking for better products to help with my health problems. I had tried about four other companies but never got the concept of network marketing.

Q: What were you doing before this?
A: I was a hair dresser for 34 years. I retired after doubling my income with Isagenix.

Q: Did you choose the direct sales model on purpose?
A: No, I was just in it for the product.

Q: How many hours per week do you work now?
A: It varies. Isagenix is a part of my life so I share it every moment I can. I do like to take weekends off, but I probably work about 60 hours a week.

Q: How about when you first got started?
A: Fewer hours then. I was only working it part time. Within a year I was working it full time and started putting in the 60 hour weeks.

Q: Do you set goals? Do you write them down?
A: Absolutely. I had a hard time in the beginning, but realized when I started building a team, I needed to set goals. I have about 10 vision boards, I like visuals.

> *"... when I started building a team, I needed to set goals."*

Q: How long did it take you to make $1,000,000?
A: Five years.

Q: What did that look like?
A: The first year I made $100,000 and it basically doubled every

ISAGENIX

year after that.

Q: Was it your intention to make $1,000,000?

A: No, but once I started sharing the product and seeing money come in, I thought, "I have to share more." The more success everyone on my team had with the product and the business, the more success I had.

> *"I believe in them, even when they do not believe in themselves."*

Q: When you first started, did you think you would be this successful?

A: No, absolutely not.

Q: What do you attribute your success to?

A: I believe in the product and the results. People have incredible life changing stories. I really connect and build relationships with people. I encourage and support the people on my team and my customers. I love people, I see their greatness. The transformations in people, whether it's weight loss, health, or financial, are so motivating to me.

Q: What techniques have you found to be successful in recruiting others?

A: I love talking to people. My specialty is connecting with others. I listen to them and listen to see if there is a need for what I have to offer. I ask empowering questions.

Q: How do you keep your team motivated?

A: I do team calls and talk to my leaders on a regular basis. I call everyone. I stay connected and coach them if they allow me to coach them. I believe in them, even when they do not believe in themselves.

Q: What have been your greatest challenges and how have you overcome them?

A: My greatest challenge has been belief in myself and belief that I could do this. I used to be a one on a scale of 1-10, now I am a 10. Since 1989, I have been heavily involved in personal growth and development. I read and listen to books all the time. I love Steven Covey, T Harv Eker, Napolean Hill, and Jim Rohn.

Q: How has making $1,000,000 changed your life?

A: Most of all it has relieved financial stress. I was sick and over-weight, and didn't have the means to contribute to the lives of others. I can have fun now and make contributions to others. I believe that giving back what I have been given is the most important thing about making a million dollars. I can assist my family with things they need, I have a new home, I can stay in alignment with integrity and come from the heart. I have retired my husband; and my daughter and son are part of my business and can both stay home with their families. The journey I have taken has been the biggest change.

> *"I believe that giving back what I have been given is the most important thing about making a million dollars."*

Q: Is there anything else you want to share?

A: There is a lot of misinformation and we are here to set it straight. It has been a roller coaster ride, not easy, but fun. You need to have patience. Direct sales and network marketing is an industry everyone should look at. We can really make a difference in people's lives. If you're passionate about why you are doing your business, you will be successful.

ISAGENIIX

"I'd tell anyone to try direct sales. It's a great way to own your own business without all the risk."
Jennifer Raybaud, Tastefully Simple

◆

BACKGROUND

Jennifer Raybaud is what some might call a natural salesperson: warm, outgoing and determined to close the deal. "When I was six years old, while other girls were playing dolls, I was going door-to-door playing the Avon lady. I absolutely love the thrill of the sale." Raybaud traded her career as a legal secretary to become a stay-at-home mother in the early 1990s. By the end of the decade, she had two children and the itch to get back into the working world. When Raybaud started with Tastefully Simple, she started like any consultant, working hard to make her $400 quarterly sales goal. Today, Raybaud is a Tastefully Simple Senior Team Mentor and her team produces nearly $6 million in annual sales. She is ranked as one of the company's top five salespeople. Jennifer is 43 years old, and lives in St. Clair Shores, MI.

INTERVIEW

Q: What year was the company founded?
A: 1995.

Q: What year did you start with the company?
A: 1999.

Q: Why did you choose this company in particular?
A: I was with another company and wasn't getting enough business. I found a lady on a "mom" chat room and we did a catalog party swap. She did Tastefully Simple and my family loved

all the stuff I ordered. I sold so much just by making and serving it to my friends and family, I thought I would supplement my income by becoming a distributor. I didn't want to do any parties, I just wanted to sell to my friends and family and make a little extra money. After about a month, I could see the potential and decided I would take it to the next level.

Q: Did you have previous experience in direct sales?
A: Yes, for over 25 years.

Q: What were you doing before this?
A: I was with another direct sales company and also worked at a law firm.

Q: Did you choose the direct sales model on purpose?
A: Yes, I fell in love with my Avon lady when I was a kid. I thought her job was the most glamorous job on the planet. She used to give me all her old catalogs, order forms, samples, etc. I would play "Avon lady" all the time. I grew up wanting to be in direct sales.

Q: How many hours per week do you work now?
A: 30.

Q: How about when you first got started?
A: More because I let my party schedule run me instead of me running it. My time was used differently, I used to do more parties, now I work with my team more.

Q: Do you set goals? Do you write them down?
A: Absolutely. I write them down and communicate them to everyone.

Q: How long did it take you to make $1,000,000?
A: Seven years.

Q: What did that look like?

A: The first year I only made $2,500. The second year it jumped to $25,000, and the third year I made $75,000. It doubled every year for the next five years.

Q: Was it your intention to make $1,000,000?
A: Yes, I wanted to have a team and I wanted what management had to offer.

Q: When you first started, did you think you would be this successful?
A: Partially. I remember saying to my husband when I was with my previous company, "I should be further along. I think I am smart enough to do better, maybe I am just in the wrong company." So I knew when I switched I was going to be successful. However, I never thought I would be making six figures, I wanted to just make $20,000-$30,000 a year as a stay-at-home mom.

> *"You have to be the consultant you want to recruit."*

Q: What do you attribute your success to?
A: Being self motivated. I know how to get over procrastination and I am willing to do the things other people aren't willing to do.

Q: What techniques have you found to be successful in recruiting others?
A: You attract what you put out there. If you want good, hard working team members who are self motivated, you need to put that out there. Be confident, lead by example, and be consistent. You have to be the consultant you want to recruit.

Q: How do you keep your team motivated?
A: I don't feel like I have that much power. No one motivates me, I motivate myself. You need to bring self motivated people into the business. I teach my team that motivation is within their control and the success of their business is up to them.

JENNIFER RAYBAUD

Q: What have been your greatest challenges and how have you overcome them?

A: Living in the state I live in (Michigan), we have been in a serious economic crisis for the past few years. I have learned to adjust. I do what I can with what I have control over. Since people are spending less money, I just know that I need more people at each party.

Q: How has making $1,000,000 changed your life?

A: It has allowed me to have choices in my life. Instead of having to buy the cheapest things because that is all I can afford, I have choices. My children go to private school which is very important to me. Also, I am not dependent on anyone. If I had to take care of myself and my kids, I could, and that gives me great peace of mind.

Q: Is there anything else you want to share?

A: You hear all the time "I've been in the business for such a long time, I should be more successful." Time served does not equal success. Just because you have been in for a long time, doesn't mean you deserve success. In direct sales, people on top are people who have waited, paid their dues, and worked their way up... key word WORK.

> *"I teach my team that motivation is within their control and the success of their business is up to them."*

TASTEFULLY SIMPLE

"The only way to fail in our industry is to quit."

Susan Sly, Isagenix

◆

BACKGROUND

Years ago, Susan Sly lost everything. Within a 16 week period, she was diagnosed with multiple sclerosis , ended her marriage, lost her business, and found herself over $100,000 in debt as a single mom. At that time, she made a decision that she would create a new life and live her full potential. She chose Isagenix as the vehicle for her success. Susan is a successful entrepreneur, author, speaker, master trainer, certified nutritional consultant, certified trainer and coach, with over 17 years of experience in health and wellness. She has generated over $50 million in sales in the industry of network marketing and become a seven figure annual income earner. Susan is the author of the bestselling books *The Have It All Woman*, *MLM Woman*, and is the co-author of the new book, *The Ultimate Guide to Power Prospecting.* She is the co-founder of the Have It All Women's Weekend where women undergo three days of life changing personal empowerment.

SUSAN SLY

[handwritten marginalia: But 1st add to get]

INTERVIEW

Q: What year was the company founded?
A: 2002.

Q: What year did you start with the company?
A: 2003.

Q: Why did you choose this company in particular?
A: I had a health and wellness background, I was a personal

> *"The last thing I do each night before I go to sleep is read an affirmation."*

trainer and did sales and marketing for Bally Total Fitness, so it made sense to stay in that industry. After a recruiter from Isagenix called me 21 times, I decided I would look at the cleansing program. I was impressed by the formulator. I knew of him from the fitness industry. I started using the products and they made sense to me.

Q: Did you have previous experience in direct sales?
A: Yes, with a few different companies. I had several negative experiences which is why it took me a while to say yes to Isagenix.

Q: What were you doing before this?
A: I owned a health club for years and then worked for Bally's.

Q: Did you choose the direct sales model on purpose?
A: Yes, I was looking for a way that I could get back on my feet and begin to empower other women. That is what drew me back into the industry. I found a product and compensation plan I could believe in.

Q: How many hours per week do you work now?
A: 30. I set a strict schedule and set office hours and I follow them.

Q: How about when you first got started?
A: Back then, I still had a full time job and worked about 10 hours a week with Isagenix. I bumped up to 20 hours when I quit my job. I then bumped up to 30 hours to retire my husband.

Q: Do you set goals? Do you write them down
A: Yes, from the very beginning. I write my goals in the present as "I am". I have them all over my walls, I have a vision board,

ISAGENIIX

affirmations written everywhere, and I have a goal book. The last thing I do each night before I go to sleep is read an affirmation.

Q: How long did it take you to make $1,000,000?
A: Three and a half years.

Q: What did that look like?
A: The first year I made $50,000, the second $190,000, third $480,000, and fourth $700,000. I now make over a million annually.

Q: Was it your intention to make $1,000,000?
A: Absolutely!

Q: When you first started, did you think you would be this successful?
A: Yes, I believed I could be. I also believe that whatever goals we set for ourselves, we will accomplish, as long as we do the work.

Q: What do you attribute your success to?
A: I was an athlete and knew how to train for success. I had faith that if I did the work, no matter what, I would be successful. I treat my business like a sport. I train and learn and grow every day. I didn't come to try, I came to succeed.

Q: What have you found to be successful in recruiting others?
A: I've done it all, but I like face to face connecting best. I find out someone's needs, goals, and dreams; and then show them how Isagenix can help them get there. I set them up for success right from the beginning.

Q: How do you keep your team motivated?
A: I have them write their goals and dreams. I reward everything they do, even the small things. I am constantly there for them.

Q: What have been your greatest challenges and how did you overcome them?

A: I had to let go of comparing myself to others and do things for myself in my own way and in my own time. I had to let go of being a perfectionist and become completely transparent in all things I do. I let my team know I am on the journey with them.

Q: How has making $1,000,000 changed your life?

A: I sponsor a trauma center in Cambodia. I travel there each year. I have always made contributions, but now they are bigger and I actually get to travel there and see the difference I am making. I also support several other charities that benefit children and women. I have more freedom and resources to travel, to give to my family, to retire my husband, and I do have some indulgences too...Prada boots.

Q: Is there anything else you want to share?

A: The only way to fail in our industry is to quit. No one is an overnight success no matter what they say. You need to do little things every day to work toward your goals and dreams. Stay consistent and patient, and you will get to where you want to be.

ISAGENIX

9

"This is not a get rich quick business. Can you get rich? Absolutely! But it's all about what you put into it."
Sherry Weaver, Passion Parties

◆

BACKGROUND

Sherry started with Passion Parties in 1999 at the age of 28 to earn a little extra money to make ends meet. She was a single mom of three with a low paying job, and it took every bit of money she made to provide for her kids. She attended a corporate event a year later and left wanting to build an empire. And she did just that. Sherry has built a dedicated and growing team and is one of the Million Dollar Club members with Passion Parties. She earns a Home Award and Car Award every month and has been honored with the Award of Excellence which has only been given to five leaders in Passion Parties. Sherry is 38 years old, and lives in Bruce, MS.

INTERVIEW

Q: What year was the company founded?
A: 1994.

Q: What year did you start with the company?
A: 1999.

Q: Why did you choose this company in particular?
A: I had been to a couple parties and they were fun and educational. A lady I worked with was having a party and I decided instead of going to the party, I would start selling the product. There were no other competing companies where I lived and I wanted to make an extra $500 a month.

SHERRY WEAVER

Q: Did you have previous experience in direct sales?
A: I had been in one company for two months, so not really.

Q: What were you doing before this?
A: I sewed decorative pillows for a furniture factory.

Q: Did you choose the direct sales model on purpose?
A: No, I had no idea what that all meant, I just wanted extra instant cash.

Q: How many hours a week do you work now?
A: 40 hours. 24 hours with my team and 16 hours doing parties.

Q: How about when you first got started?
A: Less, I was only doing parties, about 12 hours a week.

Q: Do you set goals? Do you write them down?
A: Yes, absolutely! And I do write them down, they are posted everywhere. I have dream boards, goals, and my life purpose all written and posted.

Q: How long did it take you to make $1,000,000?
A: Nine years.

Q: What did that look like?
A: My first and second year I made $10,000. I started building a team the third year and I made $50,000. It doubled every year after that.

Q: Was it your intention to make $1,000,000?
A: No, I thought making that kind of money was only for a few people and I wasn't one of them.

Q: When you first started, did you think you would be this successful?
A: No, I didn't have the desire to be this successful. But then the products were selling so easily, I started seeing more po-

tential and I was very good at the selling. I then learned to help others get what they want and realized that would give me what I want. Once I started offering this gift to others, it happened very quickly.

Q: What do you attribute your success to?

A: Being genuine and coming from the heart. On my team, I truly love each and every girl I sponsor, and I appreciate them for who they are and what they have to offer. I am very personable and that has played a huge role in my success.

Q: What techniques have you found to be successful in recruiting others?

A: Finding out what they want from the business and why they are interested in it. I make it all about them and not about me.

Q: How do you keep your team motivated?

A: I recognize my team for every little accomplishment. I also do personal coaching calls and have a lot of personal contact with them.

Q: What have been your greatest challenges and how have you overcome them?

A: Being a leader is a huge challenge, it's something I have to work at daily. To overcome it, I have had to really take the time to get to know every single one of my team members and treat them each as a business partner. I always show up and am always in "learning" mode.

Q: How has making $1,000,000 changed your life?

A: I had dropped out of high school at age 15, had three kids by the time I was 20, and was a single mom. So I always had to take lower paying jobs. Money had always been a limiter in my life. Making the money I make

> *"I recognize my team for every little accomplishment."*

SHERRY WEAVER

now has given me the freedom to do for my kids the things I never got to experience. I put all my kids through college with no student loans. I have also been able to buy each of my kids and my mom a house.

Q: Is there anything else you want to share?
A: It is so important that people realize this is not a get rich quick business. Can you get rich? Absolutely. But it's all about what you put into it. People think they can work it as a hobby and get paid as a business. You need to be self motivated. Until you take the actions to build and grow your business, you will not be successful. I also believe leaders need to dig deep and find out what a potential consultant or team member wants out of the business. Then they need to focus on helping them achieve it.

10

"When I realized that I was the one that got to decide, everything changed. When I stopped being the victim, my life changed."

Lisa Wilber, Avon

◆

BACKGROUND

Lisa Wilber has been selling products for Avon since 1981. At 18 years old, she worked her Avon business part time until 1988 when she was laid off from her secretarial job. Her Avon income dramatically increased after 1993 when she joined Avon's multi-level marketing program. She is currently the #4 money earner in the country inside the program. She has earned 21 Avon trips. Lisa is the author of *Marketing Ideas for the Wild at Heart* and owner of The Winner in You. She was the first Avon representative to be featured in an *Upline Journal* success story. Interviews have also appeared in *NH Business Review*, *Executive Female* magazine, *Home Business Connection* magazine, *Networking Times* magazine, *Avon Dreams* magazine and the book *Dream Achievers*. Lisa Wilber is a professional member of the National Speakers Association and is one of the featured authors in the books *Build It Big* and *More Build It Big* from the Direct Selling Women's Alliance where she was named the Ambassador of the Year in both 2004 and 2007. In 2007 she was given the highest honor awarded to Avon representatives by being named "Woman of Enterprise". In 2008 Lisa Wilber was named to the "Top 50 Most Influential People in Direct sales" list. Lisa is 46 years old, and lives in Weare, NH.

INTERVIEW

Q: What year was the company founded?
A: 1886.

Q: What year did you start with the company?
A: 1981.

Q: Why did you choose this company in particular?
A: I was 18 years old, married, and living in Guam. I needed to earn money and had no skills. The other military wives were selling other things and I didn't see anyone selling Avon, so I thought I would give it a try.

Q: Did you have previous experience in direct sales?
A: No.

Q: What were you doing before this?
A: I was in high school.

Q: Did you choose the direct sales model on purpose?
A: No, I didn't know anything about it. All I knew was that in Guam everything made in the USA was a big seller and no one was selling Avon.

AVON

Q: How many hours a week do you work now?
A: 30.

Q: How about when you first got started?
A: Much less, I was part time for years. I didn't know full time was a possibility. I left Guam, moved around the states working up to getting a "real job". In 1987 with the recession, I was laid off and couldn't get a job anywhere. I learned about the business part of Avon and started working it as a full time business, about 60 hours a week.

Q: Do you set goals? Do you write them down?
A: Yes, I have to see a visual. For example, when I was working on earning a car, I carried around a toy car that I had made up to look just like the one I wanted.

Q: How long did it take you to make $1,000,000?

A: The network marketing side of Avon didn't start until 1990. I started with the networking marketing in 1993. 15 years into the business, just six years after Avon went to a network marketing format, I made a million dollars.

Q: What did that look like?
A: In just the direct sales business, I made about $1,000 a year for the first six years. After 1987 when I lost job, I made $12,000 my first year, $25,000 my second, and then about $35,000 a year after that. The first year I built my team, I made $50,000. By my fourth year I broke $100,000.

> *"...I had no idea that anyone was making that kind of money in Avon."*

Q: Was it your intention to make $1,000,000?
A: When I first started, no, I had no idea that anyone was making that kind of money in Avon.

Q: When you first started, did you think you would be this successful?
A: No, but when I started building a team, I researched the company, compensation plan, and other successful distributors. Then I had a goal, "millionaire by 40". And I was!

Q: What do you attribute your success to?
A: I didn't know enough to know this would be as hard as it was, so I just did what I had to do. I was naïve and had no idea that this would be hard. I didn't know enough to quit. It was my only option so I stuck with it! I am also big into personal development. I had to become a different person to be able to handle the money and invest in myself and in my business. One book I love is *Lead the Field* by Earl Nightingale. BOOK

Q: What techniques have you found to be successful in recruiting others?

A: I didn't realize that Avon was known for knocking on doors, so when I had to go full time I looked at other retail businesses and what they were doing. What I did was find as many ways as I could to put my name with Avon's name in public, so when everyone thought of Avon, they thought of me. I do everything I can think of to get myself out there, I brand myself with the company name.

Q: How do you keep your team motivated?

A: I do a newsletter and reward top sellers and recruiters weekly. I acknowledge birthdays and special occasions. I give a lot of recognition and am in constant communication with everyone as much as I can.

Q: What have been your greatest challenges and how have you overcome them?

A: My greatest obstacle is definitely myself, and continues to be. I had ZERO self esteem when I started. I overcame that by being around people that are more successful than me so I always have something to strive for. I need to be around other people who are doing and having big things.

Q: How has making $1,000,000 changed your life?

A: I went from living in a trailer, driving a Yugo, and eating macaroni and cheese, to the way I live now. I feel empowered that I know how to earn that kind of money. It used to be a constant struggle with poverty and now I was able to adopt a daughter on my own. We've been to Disney World four times! It's a totally different life. I have so many choices with what I can do.

> *"I do everything I can think of to get myself out there, I brand myself with the company name."*

Q: Is there anything else you want to share?

A: Yes. Back then, I thought life was happening to me but I

AVON

didn't realize it was up to me, that I got to decide what my life looked like. When I realized that I was the one that got to decide, everything changed.

> *"Back then, I thought life was happening to me but I didn't realize it was up to me"*

When I stopped being the victim, my life changed. I love personal development and I love Jim Rohn! I love the smell of someone else cleaning my house.

Don't quit! When people say, "I'm going to give it six months and if something doesn't happen I'm going to quit", well that is just crazy! Would you do that with your kids? If they aren't what you want them to be in six months, would you just quit them?

LISA WILBER

APPENDIX

Build Up Your Ability to Bounce Back From Setback
by Caterina Rando, MCC

When you think about what it takes to be successful in direct selling over the long haul, you might cite a need for determination, strategic thinking, or the ability to communicate ideas effectively. While all these and other character traits will facilitate one's ability to create good results, there is another important characteristic that is often left undeveloped. That important character trait is resilience: your bounce-back ability.

In coaching and training direct sellers over the years, I've noticed that how someone reacts to what's done to them is as important as what they do. We can make detailed strategic plans, begin daily activities to move us forward, put structures in place that support us in creating what we want – but the world will always throw us unexpected changes and unanticipated events.

Betty Talmadge, an American meat broker and cookbook author, is the one who first said, "Life is what happens to you when you're making other plans." We cannot control anything or anyone else, and we create a lot of disappointment and frustration (as well as waste a lot of our life energy) when we try.

Life happens. You might have every appointment in a week cancel, or you might have no one show up for a presentation. Your new recruit that you have been coaching and cultivating for three months might decide to move to Tahiti. Your computer and its contents could be consumed by a virus. Your home could be flooded or your car stolen. At some point in everyone's life, setbacks occur.

How you respond to what happens is what will make the greatest difference for you, both personally and professionally. Your resilience is what gives you the ability to get back up after you have been knocked down — even after the second and third rounds of having your plans pummeled.

If you think your bounce back ability can use a strength-training program, follow these principles to soar through setbacks and keep your resilience revved up.

Use Your Power of Choice

Begin to look at how resilient you are in everyday occurrences. Do you let traffic, a rude comment, a delayed plane, a spilled cup of coffee, or a disappointing phone call, ruin your whole day? Or do you consciously choose to bounce right back? We do not always have a choice in what happens to us, but we always have a choice about how we react to it.

Let It Out

Talk it out with a friend, write it out in your journal, cry it out on your couch, sweat it out in the gym. Do whatever it takes to purge yourself of the emotion you feel over this setback. The bigger the setback, the longer it takes, and the more emotions you have to purge. Do not stuff feelings about the setback; acknowledge your anger, sadness, frustration or fear. Once you're in touch with those feelings, work on releasing them. A sense of closure or completion, which eventually leads to peace, is necessary in order to move forward.

Look for the Lesson

Setbacks serve. They bring with them lessons about you, about life, about relationships. When a setback erupts in your path, do not dowse the flames without first examining its lesson. Learning the lessons that your setbacks deliver to you is one of the ways you build your resilience. Prepare yourself for the next surprise by learning something from this one. Look for the lesson.

Build on Past Successes

Sometimes your setback might seem too much to handle.

There may be times you find it hard to go on, especially after the significant personal loss of a relationship or a loved one. To help yourself bounce back during such difficult times, think about other challenges that you have faced in your lifetime. Think about how you dealt with them, and how you got through them. What worked for you during those times? Was it taking a vacation, talking to counselor, watching "I Love Lucy" reruns, or taking a leave of absence from your job? Whatever it was, ask yourself if it is time to do it again.

Schedule Rejuvenation

Sometimes when we experience a setback, it can kick us into high gear. We force ourselves to try harder, work longer, do more. If setbacks motivate you to take action, that's fine, as long as it is not at the expense of your self-nurturing. Self-nurturing, the time spent rejuvenating your energy and replenishing your spirit, is more important after a setback then at any other time. Go get a massage, take a yoga class, melt in a tub of lavender suds, chat endlessly on the phone with a friend. Do whatever it is that deeply nourishes you. Make the care and feeding of yourself a top priority during times of personal challenge. It will ensure that you bounce back faster.

Ask Yourself a Powerful Question

Instead of asking yourself questions that further burden you like, "How could this happen to me?" or "What did I do to deserve this?" – ask yourself powerful questions that help build your resilience. Find ways to uplift yourself and shift your view of the situation by asking questions such as, "How can I turn things around?" and "How can I support myself during this challenging time?" Even if you don't get an answer right away, keep asking yourself these powerful questions until the guidance that will best serve you appears.

It is your ability to bounce back after setbacks that will keep you successful and fulfilled over the long haul of your career and your life. What matters is not how many times you find yourself face down in the sand, but how many times you get back up and dust yourself off. Take just one of these principles to start with, then add another and another, until resilient responses are second nature to you. As you build these skills, why not start the day with this bold affirmation: "Go ahead life, send me a setback. I eat setbacks for breakfast. They are great fuel for the day!"

Caterina Rando, MA, MCC, shows women in direct selling how to book, sell, recruit and lead with ease. She is the creator of the Direct Sales Business Breakthrough Coaching Program to accelerate your business growth. Visit http://www.directsale-scoaching.com to sign up for Caterina's free business building tele-classes, read more articles and listen to podcasts. Caterina can be reached at by email at cat@directsalescoaching.com or by phone at 1-415-668-4535.

ABOUT THE AUTHOR

Kirsten McCay-Smith comes from the fitness industry where she first learned about network marketing fifteen years ago.

She signed up with several nutrition and supplement companies over the span of her career as a personal trainer/fitness instructor. Although there were many successful people in each of the companies she signed up with, it wasn't until 2005 (when she found a company completely unrelated to the health/fitness industry) that she found success in the direct sales/network marketing industry. Her new business took off and she was able to leave her job and the fitness industry after 1 ½ years as a network marketer. She has never looked back.

Kirsten now has control over her time and finances and spends her days helping others do the same.

In 2008 she was the number one recruiter in her company and has doubled her successes in 2009. She is a national trainer and speaks to groups on how to become the people they need to be in order to get what they want in their lives. She spends much of her own time on personal development and knows her business can only grow to the extent that she grows.

You can keep up with Kirsten on her blog at:
millionaires.50interviews.com

You can also drop Kirsten an email at: **kirsten@50interviews.com**

Become a fan on Facebook and connect with other readers:
http://bit.ly/kirsten99

ABOUT 50 INTERVIEWS

Imagine a university where not only does each student get a text book custom tailored to a curriculum they personally designed, but where each student literally becomes the author!

The mission of 50 Interviews is to provide aspiring, passionate, driven people a framework to achieve their dreams of becoming that which they aspire to be. Learning what it takes to be the best in your field; directly from those who have already succeeded. The ideal author is someone who desires to be a recognized expert in their field. You will be part of a community of authors who share your passion and who have learned first-hand how the *50 Interviews* concept works. A form of extreme education, the process will transform you into that which you aspire to become.

50 Interviews is a publisher of books, CDs, videos, and software that serve to inform, educate, and inspire others on a wide range of topics. Timely insight, inspiration, collective wisdom, and best practices derived directly from those who have already succeeded. Authors surround themselves with those they admire, gain clarity of purpose, adopt critical beliefs, and build a network of peers to ensure success in that endeavor. Readers gain knowledge and perspective from those who have already achieved a result they desire.

If you are interested in learning more, I would love to hear from you! You can contact me via email at: brian@50interviews.com, by phone: 970-215-1078 (Colorado), or through our website:

www.50interviews.com/kirsten

All my best,
Brian Schwartz
Authorpreneur and creator of *50 Interviews*

OTHER 50 INTERVIEWS TITLES

Successful Property Managers
by Mike Levy
propertymanagers.50interviews.com

Dream It, Live It, Love It: 50 Athletes Over 50
by Don McGrath
athletes.50interviews.com

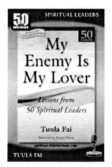

My Enemy Is My Lover: Lessons from 50 Spiritual Leaders
by Tuula Fai
spiritual.50interviews.com

50 Entrepreneurs: The Secrets to Thriving in Uncertain Times.
by Brian Schwartz
entrepreneurs.50interviews.com

CPSIA information can be obtained at www.ICGtesting.com
Printed in the USA
269772BV00003B/72/P